Brahms

SELF-SYMPHONIES

The Self-

Symphonies

Daniel Weeks

Published by BLAST PRESS
324B Matawan Avenue
Cliffwood, NJ 07721
(732) 970-8409
gregglory@aol.com
gregglory.com
amazon.com/author/gregglory

To the memory of my grandmother

Doris Waterworth Osborne

CONTENTS

SELF-SYMPHONY NO. 1   **11**

   1. Un poco sostenuto—Allegro   *13*

   2. Andante sostenuto   *19*

   3. Un poco Allegretto e grazioso   *23*

   4. Adagio—Più Andante—Allegro non troppo, ma con brio   *27*

SELF-SYMPHONY NO. 2   **32**

   1. Allegro non troppo   *33*

   2. Adagio non troppo—L'istesso tempo, ma grazioso   *40*

   3. Allegretto grazioso   *46*

   4. Allegro con spirito   *49*

SELF-SYMPHONY NO. 3   **53**

   1. Allegro con brio   *55*

   2. Andante   *61*

   3. Poco Allegretto   *68*

   4. Allegro   *72*

SELF-SYMPHONY NO. 4   **77**

   1. Allegro non troppo   *78*

   2. Andante moderato   *93*

   3. Allegro giocoso—Poco meno presto—Tempo I   *102*

   4. Allegro energico e passionate—Più Allegro   *106*

AFTERWORD: ORIGINS   **113**

ABOUT THE AUTHOR   **141**

ABOUT THE PUBLISHER   **143**

SELF-SYMPHONY NO. 1

Inspired by the
First Symphony in C minor
by Johannes Brahms

1. Un poco sostenuto—
Allegro

Mortality never leaves
        the sublime consciousness.
As he walks
        absentmindedly
through furnishings,
        thin but square-shouldered,
and happy here, my son grown nine
        reminds me of my father,
though I
        could not have known
Dad at nine.   Was he happy, his
        mother dead of a kind
of swelling, as if these
        ominous strings
and kettledrums rose up
        within her to rattle
the skull with what
        was unendurable? We heard
she lay days dazed

Dad at nine

with pain—a nurse puttering
about the white sheets
    as the little line of the oboe
stretches out
    a funeral song, on key
but out of all
    earshot.

War and unremitting strife—
    I saw four sons
heaped heavily in
    a courtyard at Ramadi,
their soles
    lifted whitely toward
the lens—this
    is the peace of
rottenness and decay.
    Shaving earlier that morning,
had they thought of this?

A better wish
would be
    a glass of beer and
sweethearts to kiss
    beneath the chiffon sound
of summer trees.

Naught holy but
    this! Is this
not what my
    saint might
say, addicted
    and rolling in
the splendor—though
    that water—fresh
and salty in its day—
    is done?

Noble anger is
    the catalyst

of useful change,
        but this
strong elixir is
        forgot—all
suffering and death
        borne with
equanimity—an
        unsymphonic
politesse.

Swelling again, the strings
        and oaks outside feel
something, but I am remembering
        my father. Have I ever
seen a picture of him at nine or only
        as a babe, wool-bonneted
and looking up from
        his wicker carriage
on the broad porch one winter
        in Ocean Grove?

2. Andante sostenuto

The cross hung up
    above the altar at
St. Mike's once seemed
    to radiate an aura
of amber light, a Danaean shower.
    I believed then
someone loved us—
    a sentiment
of granddames and foolish boys.

In the beergarten, under
    the pleasant undulant
      trees of a cool evening,
we know better now.

Can one behold a
    grandeur in
any human thing?
    Swelling lovely—

disconcerting, bold? Or do

     the footsteps of

          the gods always

     splinter all the matchsticks,

       proclaiming even

          our proclivities

            halbschürig?

Brahms—had we

     listened, we

had never

     gone so wrong. This fire

glows delicate as

     the twilight—

the one singing

     string

inviolable:

Always this!
Always this!

Our ear off,
    the song leaves
lines of starved
    unshaven men and
ribbed children
    too tired to weep amid
shattered cities
    where ragged
women creep, the sooty streets
    burned through
        with fire from
        the air.

3. Un poco Allegretto e grazioso

Some unknown one
is carried in me,
        as my father
is borne, an Old Anchises
        on my son's shoulders.

        Yet, theatricality is troublesome—
a falseness actors
        seem blind to as they
revel in art's demise.
        Costumed, the histrion
with baudy makeup
        and twisted fingers
must dismiss
        the thundershowers
of worlds even as
        his lips pronounce them.

Old Anchises

Look to that human thing!
Look to it, bloody and graven—held high
in the hard arms of Homer,
free to live
above all other things.

4. Adagio—Più Andante— Allegro non troppo, ma con brio

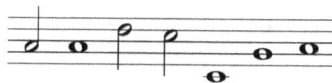

Nightcast
    and wandering
with but
    a ghost to guide me,
I can bequeath
    only chances to these
beloved, tucked
    safe into their beds,
high above the vagaries of
    the sunbaked grass
and purple dust.

Call to me,
ye gentle fathers

So many, though, have
    mercilessly died, the solemn
horn intoning
    their mourning

a ghost to guide me

song—the unwinded horn
    terrifying the morning
skies above the children
    we once were,
even as we stood amid
    light-flooded
fields of green, shouting
    the hosannahs of play,
god's clean linen light
    upon our shoulders
and haloes in our hair.

Call to me,
ye gentle fathers

The trees in the yard are
    calm now, but stand
acute to signal
    any change

in the wind's bereavement—
    a dark barrier
soft-broken, through which
    the willing eye
may glimpse the cream-sweet
    sky of
a sudden chaos.

Call to me,
ye gentle fathers

Importunate and
    ungentle,
the chattering locusts come,
    unwitnessed
even by the earth's eye,
    rolling lovely in
its unseen sea.

SELF·SYMPHONY NO. 2

Inspired by the
Second Symphony in D major
by Johannes Brahms

1. Allegro non troppo

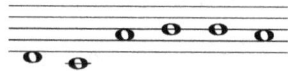

With the pewters and pale greens
        of the sea obscuring
an underlying tumult
        and the horn of the sky
bleached of its blue,
        children kick
and toss handfuls of sand and
        with the seabirds shriek
just to catch the echo.

        The haze cannot
obscure the sharp
        line of the horizon. Fortuitous
                life and its suffering
seems never forlorn. We
        carry with us the
spirit of the dead, the seed
        of the Hun
and Xiongnu, the spore of Celts

and far-flung Magyars,
recreated eyes, purposeless
as the labor of ants,
the consciousness
of multifarious suns.

Wild strings, high above
the bowing of
the bass, strings
in the shape
of cirrus clouds
in soft descent.

The sea seems closer,
the tide incoming now,
gently like the soft
fingers of care and of
humanity's fervent kiss, masking
a sinisterness.

The purposeful strides
of the oblivious,
of the crooked-kneed
and stooped, the
melting flesh and naked bellies
of tanned pashas,
whose gold wristwatches
mimic the hot sungleam—

familiar themes with
the sea so calm,
defying the strong warning
of these horns,
which Brahms first heard
silently near
the Carpathian sea.

pleasure boats

Today pleasure boats
are out with squint-eyed
        fishermen, who drink
canned beer and hope
        to hook life to its end.

The grim dance
        of the bourgeois, which
the learned once despised,
        seems all there is as
sound teaches us
        to be—undefined—
unlike the dark line
        of the sea rim,
punctuating the swells
        of strings and of
the salt sea.

        The patois of beach chairs
in bright blue and pink

outshouts the neutrality
of sand and of the dark
         eyebrows of gutted
mussel shells.

Why did I come? The music,
         like a piper cub
trailing its blue banner,
         says life careens
from tragedy
         to ridicule, the
end arriving as an unexpected
         guest beneath
the sharp cascades of the sea's
         guttural laughter
and the winsome hiccups
         of terns.

2. Adagio non troppo—
L'istesso tempo, ma
grazioso

Gulls in flight
skimming the sea surface
circle once
only to return
to perch
on the jumbled black teeth
of broken jetty rocks.

The lone horn
must sound
brazenly
against the flock.

Sleep, sleep, dear child

A sudden strong wind,
like a warm savannah
or the perfumed breath
of the huntress moon,

blows over all
    the bodiless chairs.

Sleep, sleep, dear child

Jared and Rachel love
    the wild sea, not
yet knowing
    the fearful things
it whispers.

Those silver shells
    the surf tumbles,
in which the sun
    repeats itself, are
themselves
    memorials of a strange joy.

Sleep, sleep, dear child

Sleep, sleep, dear child

I'm beginning to know
        the acrid sweat
of the aged and
        to overcome
a boy's need
        to be retouched with
a fierce and wild joy,

        to feel again
the million-fingered surf's
        cold summer touch
and the subtle minds
        of the dead, leaving
translucent singing strings
        to follow over
the rhythm of dunes.

Sleep, sleep, dear child

The kettles of
the sea curl
    strike up an epitaph.
The tide's beat strengthens,
    and the reeds pipe
sweetly before they die,
    sun-dried to fine paper.

Sleep, sleep, dear child

3. Allegretto grazioso

The metaphysics of boats
and birds—all something
        without essence—the eye
constrained by
        the known—a presumption.

Perhaps this summer day
        the curled wave
shall freeze, and I shall
        walk relieved
among the frozen gleams
        of time.

A young mother
        painting the horizon with
one finger is
        always out to show
white brushstrokes of boats
        to her astonished child—a portrait,

a seascape—a singleness in

     the museum of eternity and I

the sole living thing

     imaging—my gaze fleeing

from picture to picture

     and penetrating the picture frame.

When, I then ask,

     do we cross from glee?

4. Allegro con spirito

How do they stand
themselves, these plumed
          regiments and their
headlong rush? Is
          acceptance its
own triumph?   Did
          Brahms butter up against
the sun's strength,
          which sweetly gives
to life its saccharides just
          before incinerating
each green leaf.

Sept soldats sont en marche

          Beach chatter
and dinner plans, the quest
          to improve
bad wine with
          chill talk.

All morning
      the symphonies
of little things piled high,
      agglomerated freckles and freaks,
smiles and shells, grain
      on grain of bitter sand and
the dried rinds of oranges.

Sept soldats sont en marche

Bellybuttons of kids and
      the blue
and purple veins on
      the thighs of older women,
the serried wrinkling and sad
      striations of the overtanned. The pink
and white bob
      of the safety rope's
over-optimistic buoys.

The self-assurance
of the guards, insouciant in
        a giant's white chair, high above
the infirm swimmers, caught now
        unawares
in an outgoing tide.

SELF·SYMPHONY NO. 3

Inspired by the
Third Symphony in F major
by Johannes Brahms

1. Allegro con brio

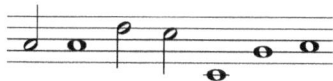

A wind out of
         nowhere
flutters cherry leaves,
         like so many
tiny green
         birds' wings,
and chases
         black-bodied
carpenter bees from
         their hoverings
near the fence rail.

         A strong
May sun
         undeterred
illuminates
         furred seeds,
which float
         in a nothingness,

black-bodied carpenter bees

as green maple

    descenders, with oily

wings, copter down

    in droves

to the blacktopped street,

    like dreamed kisses,

never to root.

I am lonely for

    you my friend,

the one who was.

Smell of leather

    gloves, the hard

feel of boned

    bats, and the ashen

color of rubberized

    baseballs

give way as

scabbed over
skinned knees
    take the field
near the woods,
    which deep
with shadows
    and leafy whispers
hold the cold
    sound of brook water
and distant traffic.

I am lonely for
    you my friend,
the one who was.

Today is lovely,
    every aspect.
There are pink
    flowers of

every shade on

    the garden

trees, and higher

    up, the oaks

summon sunlight

    in their leaves.

The cut hedge

    top across

the way reflects

    white

May fire.

I am lonely for

    you my friend,

the one who was.

2. Andante

A little lost soul
      is forever on
the bus to school.
      The dream
he trains for does
      not exist, is
already undone,
      as only
a narrator knows.
      But the bus
bumps on
      past a red
clapboard house
      he's been told
was once a country
      recruiting
post for Old Abe's
      blue coats;

Old Abe's blue coats

past Glendola School
    redolent of
dead images
    of children whose
button shoes
    have long since heaped
the refuse pile
    behind countless
isolated houses,
    their young
bodies grown
    out of shape, rotting
among blue and green
    medicinal bottles
that still catch sunlight
    when dug from
thickening mud;

             past the Christmas
tree farm
             with its smart
red barn
             so soon doomed
to suburban
             subdivision,
the trees dozed
             under and no
sign left to start
             a new sequence
of dream—countless
             kids in plaid
or pink flannel robes
             and wool-lined
leather slippers
             a-tingle with
expectation in the cold
             morning

to find papered gifts
　　　lying silent
beneath the glittering
　　　　trees—
A life lost and burned
　　　to brown,
needles and the fingers
　　　that held them
drooped, ghosted, gone,
　　　the tapestry
worn to filament, till
　　　soft wind
might tear its web,
　　　leaving nothing
but clean space.

　　　And finally red-
brick Central School,
　　　as the bus

lurches in with

    squeaking brakes,

and we

    make our way,

load on load

    of children tumbling

in and down the

    green iron stairs

to class.

3. Poco Allegretto

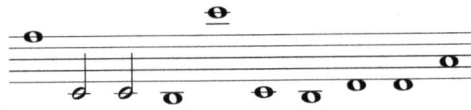

Even the dance
        is somehow somber,
the walking bass
        beneath the higher
strings and the kettledrum's
        thunderings carry
us like creek water
        to the undifferentiated
end.   Agitated
        gray miles
of water, the slow
        ghosts of old
steamers octogenarian
        eyes imposed
upon the skyline,
        their smoke
always angling back
        from
the direction of sail.

She once came

here to dance

    at the Winter Garden,

was ever kind

    to me.

The oboe

    reminds me

of golden hair

    and

an enigmatic

    smile.

Was ever kind

    to me.

The solemnity

    of a language

can never quite
        be washed
from the blood.

She was
ever kind to me.

Something German
        and melancholy
sticks like a bone
        at the core.
I admit

She was
ever kind
        to me.

4. Allegro

I wished to have
        lived a little
in every age,
        seen all the rank
thunderings
        of weather and war—
the aged father
        lifted stiff
out the farmhouse door—
        the weeping
and the sunlit
        gardens—the slick
streets of Woollcott's
        Gotham—
Sunny at the Winter
        Garden, *Ripples*,
The Sidewalks of
        New York,

with the crook-nosed
    hoofer
Lester Hope and
    silk-legged
Tiller Girls—
    Booth and Irving
on the London stage—
    Young Coleridge
with long, wet hair
    ducking in his river cave—Shelley
sending up
    balloons of revolt
and later, Byron
    standing by
a stormy sea
    with eyes pinned anxious
on the waves.

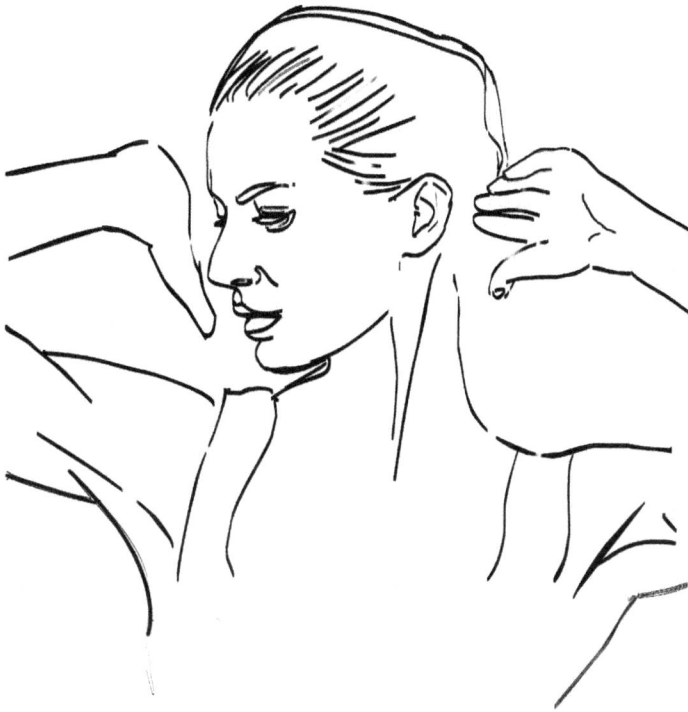

silk-legged Tiller Girls

What can flow
	with the force
of fever from
	a hot core
to be set flaming
	in wind?
One such proclaims
	a liberty to
the coal-blackened swarm,
	Leviathans
of flesh whispered
	under—heaving with
the remorseless earth,
	wailing with
plains grass and
	woodland trees,
gasping with the hiss
	of waves
along the deserted shore.

SELF·SYMPHONY NO. 4

Inspired by the
Fourth Symphony in E minor
by Johannes Brahms

1. Allegro non troppo

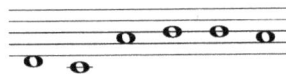

We've left off lingering in
Little Silver now, on our way
        to Red Bank—new train cars on
an old line, penetrating collapsed
        worlds and remembered sunshine,
the pupil blinking
        away the hard light of morning, trying
just to *be* decently
        while heaped high with
the ridicule of dunces and
        a future of wasted time.

The sun reproduces itself in miniscule
        in the windows of parked
cars at Matawan, and minutes later,
        having lost that metallic landscape,
we pass the green marsh where
        a large and mysterious bird
is just lifting off—heavy-winged in air.

To the east, the bay lies softly blue like
      Bristol Channel seen
from high atop the Quantocks, though
      this scene too soon gives way
to dead white birches, stark
      as starved angels, which stand
upright near the blackened tracks.

The passengers, oblivious, repeat
      themselves in
the dull loops of commerce
      until we stop—South
Amboy—in view of an
      overhanging rear deck
festooned in flowers near
      Frango's Barbecue.

The somber face of the church
        glowers in staid
and faded brick, and nearby,
        old concrete overpasses
wear penitently the ash stains of
        their destinies.

Then suddenly, the blue expanse
        of the Raritan greens
itself as it comes closer
        to the eye, giving way
in quick succession to
        the Rhodesian colossi of
Parkway bridges, like
        secret roads of pallor,
and we pass over our own
        unseen colossus toward
the freight yard and its
        spools of shiny steel.

Soon a concealed theme is
    revealed: wrecked cars
quietly sandwiched
    in the junkyard, and
as we enter the long tunnel
    beneath Hudson's river,
I ask: How do I make my dented self
    beautiful
with this old pencil?

After traversing another time
    the familiar track,
overlaid with diminished
    visions of lost trips,
and after entering again this city, itself layered
    in mildews and the sodden
leaves of buried lives,
    what does wisdom say
but to deny the millennia unlived?

I feel a rush of thickened minutes
        throbbing my temple
in some disconcert with
        the slow tug of the tunneled train,
this cult of me used
        too many times, the atrophy of muscle
striding into ignominy
        with pitiful trophies strumpeting for
one wet dollar.

        We escalate in slow motion
from the penumbraed underground
        into the city sunscape. Reality—
the Pennsylvania
        Hotel, a ragged man covered
in drifts of old newspapers,
        a long line of yellow cabs,
a young girl in
        red stockings.

a young girl in red stockings

Still,

     time quickens as one
returns to this city
     with its interfering
beat, an interruption in a desperate flow,
     more constant than traffic,
       more deadly earnest
than insistent taxi horns and sirens
     signaling anonymous emergencies.

In this city, annoyed
     businessmen stride
down 7ᵗʰ Avenue, their
     suits too much for the sun.
And weary women hammer
     the hard sidewalk
in too-high heels.

But in the bar with cold
    liquid gold in green bottles,
all is cool and insouciant,
    like the calm smile of a bedmate or
birdsong on a warm morning,
    and it comes:

The pizzicato tiptoeing like
    a child, but to a
greater precipice and no more
    eyes than an egg to see
the final figure. I wonder the while:

Am I content at fifty,
    witnessing the imploded architecture
of friends lives and dreams held
    gelatinous at
a distance—full freighters
    dim on the horizon

moving dispassionately toward

    the gone.

Brahms by this time

    was full of tricks, wearing

his rich soundscapes,

    thinking of place, but somehow

retaining a boyish joy

    beneath a fulsome beard

and weary paunch.

Pizzicato of youth seemed

    joyously forever, while

the burnishing of strong sunlight shows

    dirt and wrinkles

but little of my unkempt wish

    to be more polished than

I am.

Here joy blends with
        the resonant deep strings
of deadliest earnest—
        the music living in
the dream of itself
        as I have lived too long
untouchable—a
        necessary phase.

Is the horn always
        the premeditated sound
of the modern and
        the woodwinds, the
antique—a dusty
        nostalgia?

In this city,
        beneath repeated billposts
and tempered glass, beneath

neon, aluminum,
and asphalt, in lungs
of copper, iron,
and stone, Brahms' time
still breathes,
conveyed in the languid strings
as taxis hustle by
and people, exhausted in the heat,
seek some haven
on Minetta Lane, purposefully
striding toward the dark unknown
and afternoon martinis,
which capture refracted faces
and the bright movement
of legs beyond the windows.

An undecipherable something undercuts
the unfathomable strings and learned
ennui of the older Brahms, when suddenly

his vigor reprises itself—but it is never
enough to win the winsome girl,
    so young and eager to be kissed, yet
sensing the patina of death.

I'm wondering where one can get a stiff
    drink and some silent space in this city, with
the hurly-burly of, of, of
    the hurly-burly of voices linked desperately
by cell
to avoid the real of ALONE.
    Yet, where else can beauty reside? I saw
the hopeful eyes in Stowey, a love
    of self.

Brahms brings a dangerous
    nothingness. Life
is, after all—
    dissonant

horns against

    a mellowness of cellos

and the too sanguine flights

    of violins—

a memory of youth—like

    his lullaby—cartoonish

and infantile—crashing

    against the bulkhead

of itself.

    Here the taxis queue,

tail-lights cinglant red

    in a dance of brightnesses.

And these horns, one might suppose, prefigured

    the step-by-step descent

to conflagration by which images

    arise: The woeful woman

shouting into her phone

    on 7th: "Don't call

me anymore"—the angry man

    with his Hefty Bag of misery

screaming "Shit!" to no one

    as if his flesh

were on fire, scaring

    tourists in Chelsea

just by the sweat

    of his lip. This is

New York—

    dingy in daylight, with hieroglyphs

of stamped soot

    and old gum gone black

on the sidewalks as seas of sweaty

    humanity curse and drive

the pistons of themselves toward

    an evaporating dream—vast, lovely.

2. Andante moderato

Can ghosts glimmer, or
    do they palely shine, like
a streetlamp seen
    at a distance through a deep autumnal fog?

Brahms enlists the deep bronze horns
    of the hunt, which fade
as the overloud noise of the now obscures all
    thoughtfulness—and I relive a history
    of my own bones,
dissectible
    and rich.

    Perhaps the brassy color
of old sassafras leaves
    shall lead me to my grave.
The feet of dreamed and dreaming mourners
    shuffling through the piled
lightness caught favorably in

old sassafras leaves

a November sun, brightened—
a warmth of color beneath
a chilled wind as light
hearts bear me or the stuff of me down
a fresh-strewn path.

Hope comes in the youthful step
of a girl in orange sneakers
or in the smile of a quiet waitress, late
from Hainan, learning orders
in English and bearing in elegant white hands
a vodka martini
come wondrous in a cold
stemmed glass with a base
a bit chipped in use.

I make no claims.
I hoped.
I made a thing or two,

and I strove—
        as resonant as
an old sinew,
        as colorful as strips of
pemmican tied like new ensigns
        to the chief's chair.

But for now
        I'll have
                the duck,
orange slices,
        beer and
                fortune cookies
                        safely cellophaned,
and ask questions of
        myself, as I watch
        the faces
of women pass by
        this wide window:

A woman with
      intense eyes and
a blue silk blouse;
      three girls,
their feet earnestly sandled;
      the handsome mother
hurrying her daughter
      through just another day,
and then this
      waitress
just from China,
      quiet and lovely
with elegant
      white hands. Does she
wish like all these
      other girls
to be loved?

The productions
            of love—is
this what God
            is saying
through Brahms—
            a mind trained
to the uttermost
            to perish?

Pull me up, yon Brahms—
            these dried embers lay about,
a parcel of the same that, note-filled
            and crosslegged, rode
the train from Semmering
            to hear the prating folk poet.

I, though, wished to stand
            ceremoniously
outside the forest

and field—divine

beside the track—because

becoming

took

a lifetime to learn.

Now, I'm journeying beyond

the sun—stationary as a stone

on the whirl

and hurly-burly,

mucking up the gears,

a human thing

ringed in

black, acrid smoke

and the caved-in roofs

of abandoned factories—

witness

the sunlight
        playing all about
but never in me now
        as I spin a ponderous
shadow on the floor.

Be gone thou
        and thy striving—
the cult of the caught—
        the pulse
under a softening flesh,
        a lost
diary of sounds
        beneath the brocade of the fall:
interferences, interruption, fracture.

3. Allegro giocoso—Poco meno presto—Tempo I

Light dances
        when intermitted
by the leaves,
        themselves caught
in a chaos sublime—the moved
        and moving.

Maybe we shall dance,
        friend, as we did,
ridiculous
        with storm clouds
on our shoulders
        and earnest brown
puddles rippling
        our eyes.

But the forecast
        is for
snow.

As the temperature plunges
        and discs of clear
ice appear in
        the unflowering pots,
tears form without
        the need to cry,
the aged fly to Florida,
        and squirrels
seem frantic
        to break in.

There is a music loosed,
        thoughtless and profane,
tearing at the sky and leaving
        a film over
all that nature
        strives to be, as
the wind beats shrill cymbals
        in heaven's ears
and swells the high

          violins of
bare hickory tops.

Out in the chill January night
          the cold fingers of
this wayward wind slap
          wine-warmed cheeks
and we—forewarned—
          behold again the stars.

4. Allegro energico e passionate—Più Allegro

Shall I write
        my requiem
to these obstreperous
        horns
and somber, damned bassoons?

Shall I die
        erect
in a whirl
        of chaos immense
and thunderous—
        the last breath singing
sharp and songfully
        a new birth?

Splash and orisons—
        pain reminds:
"Stay young in summary."

Across the world the new
      come aborning
like all forgotten
      leaves, lucky if
a stone is left
      atop *their* burial mound.

The earth, fecund,
      produces
at the sun's
      behest
vigorous and
      wicked life
in mice
      and squirrels
wildcats, onions,
      goldenrod,
and buttercups—
      Queen Anne's
lace

Queen Anne's lace

                    and then
our striving
              to be swallowed,
too, anon.

Filmed legions—refugees
              in black and white—pour
out along the road in torrents
              toward France
on the silent TV screen so soon after
              a hundred celebrities in hats. So Brahms wrote
a score for the menaces to come,
              the sober note that chaos
awaited, velvet-robed,
              just beneath the lid, as the flame
of the overcivilized
              scorched hotter with intention
than any lightning strike.

Oh, but nature's fire, so distant

    and failing, makes a lovely dancing light

across this page as if I wrote

    the cursive of a new dream

upon movement, flow upon

    flow until

the ink gives out—the eye

    of all:

Cry awake and strike.

    Cry awake and strike.

Be.

AFTERWORD: ORIGINS

Brahms, Self-Symphonies, and Pots

"Boredom is a great motivator," Ralph Peterson, Jr., said to me back in 1990 when I first went to him to study drums. My playing had become stale, and I had been falling back on the same licks time and again. By May 2003, I had a similar feeling about the poetry I was writing. I was rolling out the same vocabulary, the same images, the same ideas, like Yeats's tired circus animals. I needed new inspiration and a new language. For some reason, which is still not very clear to me, I turned to Johannes Brahms, more specifically to his Third Symphony, to see if it might lead me in a new direction.

I had, of course, always known about Brahms as one of the great art-music composers of the nineteenth century, but only as a name. Outside of his ubiquitous lullaby, which had worked its way into popular culture, I really knew nothing about his music until one evening in April 2002, when my wife, Jackie, and I went to hear the New Jersey Symphony under the baton of Hugh Wolff at the Count Basie Theatre in Red Bank, New Jersey. The bill opened with Aaron Copeland's "Music for Theatre" and closed with Beethoven's "Fourth Symphony." Sandwiched between was Brahms's "Double Concerto for Cello and Violin."

We had really come to hear the Beethoven, his most classical and sedate symphony, which Schumann had called "a slender Grecian maiden." We expected it, like all of Beethoven's symphonies, to be great, so long as it was performed well, and it was. Copeland's works were good, too, but the Brahms I found to be extraordinary in every way. Here was a surprise— something new and beautiful to contemplate. Within a week, I had bought a recording of it—performed by the Chicago Symphony with Isaac Stern and Yo-Yo Ma.

My enthusiasm for the "Double Concerto" led me to seek out other works of Brahms, and I soon had in hand a recording of the complete symphonies by the Berliner Philharmoniker under the direction of Herbert von Karajan. By May 2003, then, I was much more familiar with the music of Brahms than I ever had been before, and when I needed new inspiration for my poetry, perhaps it was only natural to turn to him. I decided that I would try to write a poem while listening to one of his symphonies. The idea was to allow the music and the visual imagery around me to color what I was writing. The only rule was that, for the first draft at least, I could write only while the music was playing, for the duration of a whole symphony, and when it ended, the writing too would end. For reasons that now elude me, I began this experiment with Brahms's Third Symphony, writing my companion self-symphony while listening to it in the living room of our home in Eatontown, New Jersey, and looking out the big paned window that so beautifully frames the front gardens and tall oaks.

This first experiment seemed to work. The music brought with it a new vocabulary, and the shifts in the music—rhythmic, melodic, harmonic, and dramatic—occasioned shifts of thought and imagery in the poem. But in spite of the success of this experiment, I had not yet decided to write a series of self-symphonies, and I would not begin to write another Brahms-inspired piece for another three years.

But before that I *would* write another self-symphony. This time, though, the inspiration came in the form of a dream. This extraordinarily vivid dream— of a dead rabbit half-buried in orange loam—took place in Philadelphia in November 2003 and led to this draft of a poem, in which the rhythm was as yet slightly off-kilter:

> I saw a rabbit part way underground.
> Spring damps and a harsher winter weather
> had turned its flattened ears to blackened leather
> and its single open eye a darker brown.
>
> One shovel thrust carved its body into earth—
> to come to dust seemed the whole meaning
>   of its birth.

To this I appended the further notes:

See it in life
then as object.

A sense of touch and of disgust
    as dream fingers brush the leather ears.

I happened to be in Philadelphia with Jackie and
the kids to attend the annual craft show of the
Philadelphia Museum of Art, one of the world's most
prestigious craft exhibitions, where a friend, Karen
Downing, was exhibiting her pottery as one of twenty-
five British guest artists. Karen had grown up in the
same town as I had on the central New Jersey Shore and
graduated from the same high school, so we are very near
contemporaries in time and space. But since high school,
time and space had interceded to separate us in
significant ways. We had not seen each other in twenty
years, and she had lived in England since 1985, while I
had remained, more or less, in place. Under the
circumstances, it is tempting to interpret the dream of
unearthing the rabbit as digging into the past and the
shovel's desecration of the rabbit's body as a kind of
warning that carving into the past risks irrevocably
damaging something sacred. But none of these weighty
interpretations occurred to me at the time, and even now
the connection of the dream to seeing a schoolmate
seems to me far-fetched.
    The craft show proved an efflorescence of

exuberant postmodernism. Jewelry, metalwork, and clothing took on strange and exotic forms, some of the work approaching the gothic. Even the furniture—much of which was not too far removed from the modernistic—was oddly shaped and lacked the symmetry one generally associates with the old high modernism. And everything was brightly colored—bright blues and oranges being most prevalent. Even the woodcarvings were stained these colors. Wooden cups and vases in this way seemed more like ceramics.

As we meandered down the aisles past the many booths of the artisans, I heard Karen call out "Danny Weeks!" I was a bit taken aback by this—first, because no one but my family had addressed me by the diminutive since high school and second, because it was said in what was to my ears a distinct British accent. I was surprised to find, though, that except for the accent, Karen did not seem much changed to me. She seemed as young as when last we met, though her hair, cut fairly short, was a little darker—a light blondish brown. It had been perfectly blonde when we were in high school. The way her hair was cut, an angle of it obscured her face when she looked down—like a bird's wing—adding a refined edge to her natural beauty, through which a sharp intelligence has always shone. She stood in the same way she always had, which is something peculiar to her, with her feet slightly apart and straight forward. She was still very slender, which has always tended to give an impression from a distance that she is short of stature. But when one is closer to her, one finds she is surprisingly tall, which is an effect I recalled from before, and has the effect of a metaphor.

Karen was dressed tout en noir, and her booth was curtained in black, as were all the other booths, and on the tables, which were also clothed in black, she had her ceramics attractively displayed. But in contrast to most of what we had experienced at the show up to that point, Karen's work eschewed color and kept to what on the surface, at least, seemed regular forms. These were her "modulor" sets—pure white ceramic, the pots nesting within pots in concentric circles. The name "modulor," of course, instantly connected Karen's work with that of the high-modernist architect Le Corbusier, whom she credits as a strong influence.

At first blush, then, one is apt to see Karen's pottery as high-modernist, with its proverbial "less-is-more" style and its geometric (one might even say "scientific") symmetry and regularity. But there is this difference: While high-modern architecture emphasized scientific precision and its elements were machine-made, Karen's work is all handcrafted. Her ideal is to make her pots as precisely geometric as she can, but the variability of the human touch in her work is invariable. This means that, on closer inspection, scientific precision gives way to the unique and varied shapes whirled from the hand of a single human being—from the hand of my friend Karen Downing no less!

Thesis: My Connection to High Modernism

In Karen's art, I find an interesting dialogue between the ideal and the real, between what an artist can strive for and what can be achieved in reality. And insofar as her work begins with the scientific precision and minimalism of the high-modernist ideal, it is perhaps worth asking what this ideal represents. Although modernism dates back to the very beginning of the twentieth century and had its advent in the rejection of late Romanticism—high modernism emerged in the 1930s, during the age of the totalitarians. But it really reached its zenith after the fascists had been vanquished. From the late 1940s to the early 1960s, high modernism in architecture, known as the "International Style," was in vogue for structures attempting a certain kind of high-minded idealism. These would include the United Nations building in New York and the government buildings in Brasilia, the then-new capital of Brazil. These buildings had only recently been built when Karen Downing and I were little kids, and it would have been natural for our generation to have seen them as the precursors of a new, more promising world.

The International Style gave up almost all ornamentation, but especially any that might be connected to any one particular culture. In its place, was geometry and scientific engineering, which some found a bit cold. The ideal behind this art was to exalt "the culture of the whole," as the American historian William Graebner has expressed it, and to suppress any reference to the many distinct cultures into which humanity has divided itself. In the immediate wake of the Holocaust and a vastly destructive world war that might be seen as a competition for the domination of one culture over all others, the message of high modernism was that the rather provincial cultures with which most people associate themselves are just so much claptrap and superstition, that human beings are all essentially the same, and what holds them together is the ability to reason. Since, in the view of high-modernist idealists, the highest expression of reason is math and science, architecture and art, too, ought to exemplify these human attributes only. Anything else would be decadent. This was a high-minded attempt to get past the cultural chauvinism that had led to World War II and to the Holocaust. The political expression of this ideal was, of course, The One World of Wendell Willkie, among others, which seemed to require a unified world government. The first bold step toward creating such a government was, naturally, the establishment of the United Nations, soon ensconced in a building that is an exemplar of the International Style.

But like any good intention, "high-mindedness" can lead us blithely down dangerous byways. Indeed, it often takes us so far into the ether of our dreams that we become anesthetized to our own faults. This seems to have been the case with the postwar internationalists, who soared so deeply into their cloudy heaven that they could not see they were in danger of becoming the very thing they hated most—cultural imperialists. One whose vision was unclouded was Frank Lloyd Wright, who thought the design for the UN building a "sinister emblem for world power." Unlike the International-Style architects, Wright's modernism—which took its cue from the American landscape rather than from pure geometry—strove to be an expression of American culture as he—an American after all—understood it.

Certainly, high modernism, particularly in its Internationalist phase, was elitist—its aim, to sweep away any sentimentality that people might attach to national cultures, or, indeed, to any culture that sought to set itself apart from the culture of the whole. Now, elitism in and of itself is not always such a bad thing as it is made out to be, and I am not, in general, opposed to elitism in the arts. After all, some judgment must be made. Otherwise, every household, indeed every structure, would be an eclectic hodgepodge decorated with the painting of dogs playing poker next to a Jackson Pollock print. Come to think of it, American towns are very much this way—ill-sorted collections of tired-looking, uninspired buildings with perhaps something worthwhile left over from the nineteenth century stuck in the middle like a Praxiteles cast upon a dung heap.

But while elitism of a certain kind can serve a useful turn, politicized, enforced elitism is always ill-advised. If people cannot be convinced and educated, they still do have the right to follow their own, perhaps mistaken, ideas. Then, too, sometimes in following what to the elitist might seem an unfruitful path, they do discover or invent something useful or beautiful. So while I can admire the idea that we belong to a common humanity, the imposition of such a political ideal through one-world government and of its cultural expression through government-sponsored architecture and art seems to me too much.

Antithesis: Multiculturalism and the Problems of Self

By nature most people are extremists, especially those who are most vocal in denouncing extremism. So naturally, the high modernists, in their protest against the One-Worldism of the fascists, constructed their own extreme one-world fantasy. Critics of the International Style and of high modernism in general, especially in the United States, soon opposed to it their own ideology—multiculturalism, which is still the buzzword of the day. The multiculturalist idea is that each particular nation, ethnicity, gender, and religion has its own culture, and that far from being claptrap, as the high modernists argued, each culture is an important expression of "a people," so that each national, ethnic, gender, and religious culture should be equally valued. In this way, no one culture could be singled out, as had Judaism for instance in World War II, for erasure. In short, this left a choice of two extremes: high modernism, which proposed the erasure of all national and ethnic cultural signifiers, and multiculturalism, which at first held that all national and ethnic cultures had to be equally valued and celebrated and, therefore, folks who belonged to one particular culture had no right to criticize any other particular culture.

As multiculturalism rose to its now ascendant position, high modernism began to winnow away. But multiculturalism has its own problems, the chief of which is so obvious that it would be embarrassing to point it out were it not for the fact that, in general, people seem blind to it. People don't associate themselves with a religion, a culture, a political party, or even a baseball club in order to value and appreciate the equality of others in different groups. They associate themselves with these groups to assert their superiority to outsiders, whether they are willing to say so or not. This even applies to the multiculturalists generally, who as a group are quite forward in claiming moral superiority over those who are not so sold on the idea.

Another difficulty with the philosophy of multiculturalism is that the groups into which people are divided are somewhat abstract and arbitrary. It is difficult for many, if not most, people to determine to which culture they truly belong, as the following example will illustrate. A few years ago when my daughter was in summer camp, she had the benefit of what seemed, on the surface at least, a very diverse class. There were African-American Buddhists, Chinese Christians, and the perhaps more conventional Hispanic, Italian, and Irish Roman Catholics, European-descended Jews, and Protestants of different varieties, just to name a few distinct "types." And yet, in terms of their day-to-day lives as Americans, there seems to have been little difference among them. For most of the year, they listened to the same pop tunes, watched the same television shows, went to the same movies, and attended the same or similar schools. It was only on various ethnic and religious holidays that they perhaps diverged to any great degree.

One day my daughter came home with a form to fill out that was meant to help the camp celebrate the ethnic, religious, and cultural diversity of the kids. The form was crafted to encourage the kids to understand and take pride in their "culture," whatever they thought that was. It was clear that parents were supposed to aid the kids in completing it, but I decided to let my daughter fill it out on her own, since that seemed to me the best gauge of what her culture was. Here's how she negotiated it:

Nationality: *American*
Language: *English*
Music: *Earth, Wind & Fire and Jingle Bells*
Holidays Celebrated: *Hanukah, Christmas, and Halloween*

Special Foods: *Turkey and Pizza*

I couldn't think of a more accurate assessment of my daughter's true culture at that moment, so we turned in the form as it was. Unsurprisingly, it was not very impressive to the camp administration, which used these forms to put up displays of African sculpture and cloth; Chinese porcelain and fans; various Mexican recipes and art work, and so on. All of these displays were beautiful and interesting, but there was no display of pizza recipes and Earth, Wind & Fire CDs.

In spite of these criticisms, I don't mean to suggest that either high modernism or multiculturalism is altogether without value. High modernism and its "culture of the whole" has the virtue of leading us to at least think about our common humanity, while multiculturalism encourages us to appreciate the wonderful diversity of human culture. And yet, even though they are opposed to one another, high modernism and multiculturalism share a common problem that makes it difficult to take them seriously in philosophical terms. They each fail to come down from their idealism to connect with what is real—the individual. In the various forms of multiculturalism, the individual is only valued in connection to the ethnic, national, gender, or religious culture with which he or she associates. The individual who doesn't fit neatly into an approved package is essentially beyond the pale. The high modernist, by contrast, values only the individual who has shed the "false" chauvinism of his or her particular culture and become the approved cosmopolitan self of the culture of the whole. But this culturally naked self seems phony, too. As Coleridge astutely observed, there is no cosmopolitan self. The self, he noted, cannot be understood "apart from the elements that bething it." It is always constrained by space and time and painted with the colors of its own experience, which make each individual distinct. Cosmopolitanism is, then, as Coleridge says, the abnegation of the individual self.

An Artistic Synthesis

If there were a cosmopolitan self, Karen Downing would be close to it. She spent roughly half her life on the Jersey Shore and the other half in England. She went to college in Washington, D.C., was an apprentice potter in North Carolina and New England, and hitch-hiked all through North Africa, where she had first discovered that she wanted to be a potter after having observed the work of African masters. She seems always on the move, e-mailing about a Cy Twombly exhibit in Berlin, attending a wedding in Limousin, making a brief circuit of the East Coast of the U.S. or visiting her mom in Arizona. Her once distinct South Wall, New Jersey, accent is now effaced by the accents of the English, though she says the English themselves regard her accent as American. At the craft show in

Philadelphia, she confessed that she felt like a fraud to be included among the visiting British potters. She didn't fit quite neatly into the group.

Karen's work *does*, however, reflect her thoughtful engagement with the ideal of high modernism, but, unlike either high modernism or its opposite (multiculturalism), her art also engages with the real—the individual—the thing that really exists. She attempts to reproduce the geometry and precision of the high-modernist style, a geometry that is not really cosmopolitan, but rather, as Coleridge would say, "universal" in its reasoned appeal to our common humanity. And yet, Karen's ceramics deviate widely from a scientific geometry. The slightly wavering line of each pot rim records a moment that one individual has uniquely experienced in time and space. The line of each pot lip seems to have reeled off of Karen's finger tips, revealing the inexact geometry of its beauty. It is the pale abstract of an ideal rendered real and utterly individual. And indeed, in her mind, there is a definite connection between the slightly undulating lines of her ceramics and her own highly individualized identity. "At the heart of my work," she says, "is a childhood spent on the Atlantic coast of New Jersey. Here was a sense of scale both intimate and infinite. On the wide white sandy beach with its far horizon, in the reed beds of the estuary, in the weathered clapboard buildings and faded driftwood, there was a feeling made physical, of a slow but steady transformation."

My encounter with Karen Downing and her work caused me to wonder what elements had bethinged me. I soon found, however, that questions along these lines were not so easy to answer. If I attempted to fall back on ethnicity, problems immediately presented themselves. Like most Americans, my background is diverse. I'm English, Irish, Scottish, Welsh, German, slightly French, and a smidge Italian. Ultimately, like everyone else, I'm descended from someone who lived in Africa 150,000 years ago. My wife is Jewish, of Austrian and Russian descent, so my immediate family is even more ethnically varied than I am myself. Truth be told, I don't really feel connected in any strong way to any of these groups. My closest ethnic affinity, I suppose, is to the English. I'm about seventy-five percent English. But to which English am I connected? My earliest English ancestors to come to North America arrived aboard the *Mayflower*. But the latest to arrive was my grandmother, who came over from Preston, Lancashire, in 1925 as a Tiller Dancer to perform in Jerome Kern's musical "Sunny" on Broadway. She was half Irish, her mother's family Roman Catholic. Perhaps my closer affinity to the English side of my ancestry is simply explained by the fact that my grandmother was always present in my life as I was growing up, with her strange English-American accent. She took me to England when I was six, and I met my English cousins—but, in spite of these experiences, I have never felt particularly English in anyway. I have always felt American—dyed in the wool.

In terms of religion, my forebears were Puritans, Separatists, Anglicans or Episcopalians, Presbyterians, and Roman Catholics. I went to the Episcopal Church in my home town as a kid and was confirmed there, and I would still give a nod to its historical significance in my life. But I also attended Bible classes at the Methodist Church in Ocean Grove, New Jersey, when I was a teenager, and my most recent connection to religion has been attending various kinds of services, particularly weddings and funerals, in different synagogues in New York and New Jersey. Like Edmund Wilson, my own sense is that George Bernard Shaw had it right when he said, "At present there is not a single credible established religion in the world." If, as Wilson asserts, "religion is the cult of a god, or gods, conceived in supernatural terms," I have very little of it. The best I can say is that I believe with John Locke that if something exists now, something must have existed from all time, but I am not prepared to say definitively, as Locke seems to be, that the preexisting something is a conscious being called "God." The most I will say is that it seems likely that what we perceive as the universe emerged from a thought or dream.

Oddly, though we were not particularly close friends in high school and though I hadn't seen Karen Downing in twenty years, I had the feeling, as one somehow does with the people one grows up among, that we knew each other in some fundamental sense which is difficult or almost impossible to achieve with the people one meets later in life. This was the more curious to me because of the profound differences in our later experiences. Growing up on the Jersey Shore with the great gray Atlantic's monstrous beauty always before us is what, perhaps, most fundamentally colored who we are. I had a similar experience when I interviewed some Asbury Park police officers for a scholarly piece I was writing on the Asbury Park "race riots" of 1970. Two of the officers had lived in Asbury's West End during what they called "the troubles." The three of us were roughly the same age, and "the troubles" had been one of the most significant events of our childhood, even though we had experienced it in different ways. I was a white kid from an almost exclusively white suburb a few miles outside the city, and they were African-American kids who had lived in the black section of Asbury, much of which had been on fire during the riot. The closest I had been to the troubles themselves was to watch the state police in their riot gear form up their ranks in the neighboring town of Ocean Grove before they marched into Asbury. My interviewees, by contrast, had been right in the thick of things. But while we talked, I began to realize that in spite of our differing perspectives on this event, we understood one another in a deeper way than was possible with "outsiders." I got the same sense when I went into Pete 'n' Elda's pizzeria in Neptune, New Jersey, not too, too long ago, even though I hadn't been there in fifteen or twenty years. The longtime customers spoke in the way I spoke, and I felt a kinship that seems impossible to put my finger on or to express in any concrete way. These are my people, and whatever our culture is, it is rapidly disappearing as newcomers flood into Wall Township, Neptune, and Asbury Park, even if for the time being it persists with us somehow as a leaven wherever we go and whatever later experiences we might have.

As the foregoing attests, falling back on the usual categories of ethnicity or religion, as the multiculturalists are wont to do, does not seem to help me in defining my position in the world or even to easily identify the elements that make up my individual self. No doubt, there are elements that have influenced me more than ethnicity or religion. I am proud to be a direct descendant of at least seven veterans of the American Revolution, and I take the sometimes contending ideals of liberty and equality for which they fought seriously. Other key cultural markers include music, philosophy, and literature. Important musical influences would be Art Blakey and the Jazz Messengers, Ahmad Jamal, Thelonious Monk, Charlie Parker, Miles Davis, John Coltrane, Ralph Peterson, Jr., Tito Puente, Beethoven, Edgar Varèse, and lately, Brahms. But I've also been influenced by pop music, for instance by the bands Chicago and the Allman Brothers. My moral and political understanding has been significantly shaped by any number of philosophers, but the most important are

Socrates, Plato, Aristotle, Plotinus, Locke, Berkeley, Hume, Rousseau, and Jefferson, but even more strongly by Confucius, Thoreau, and Coleridge. The writers that have most affected me are, again, Coleridge and Thoreau, but also Homer, Shakespeare, Keats, Yeats, Poe, Longfellow, Hart Crane, William Carlos Williams, Robert Frost, Amiri Baraka (his early work), Louise Glück (in her early work), Dorothy Livesay, Robert Pinsky, Edmund Wilson, F. Scott Fitzgerald, Ernest Hemingway, and William Faulkner. Art, too, has been an important influence, particularly the works of da Vinci, Titian, Van Gogh, Picasso, Matisse, Magritte, and Pierre Bonnard, but most especially those of Cezanne.

Still, though all of these people and their works have influenced me and have been in some way incorporated into whatever it is that constitutes the self, they are not in themselves the self, nor do they suit me to belong to any particularly recognizable group. In any case, if I did fit into any group, I would immediately seek a means of escape, since to belong in such a way seems limiting. I suppose I've learned from Coleridge that the self is never static. It is always becoming something new, so that the self I am becoming always seems much more interesting to me than the self I've been. These old, past selves, in fact, always seem a little alien to me, if not slightly embarrassing. And yet, one of the reasons I write poetry is to register, consciously and unconsciously, this "ever-arriving river" of the self, as Gregg G. Brown has expressed it. At the same time, the poems, as I shape them, shape me—the poet becoming himself, as Thoreau has noted, through his work.

While some influences are fleeting, others seem persistent, in spite of the constant change the self experiences. One of the many persistent influences in my life is modernism, even high modernism, and seeing Karen Downing's work made me wonder why we two, having grown up on the Jersey Shore in semi-rural Wall Township, would find this now rather obsolete vision so appealing. My own thought, though Karen may disagree, is that it might be a form of nostalgia for something we never had. The high-modernist vision of the world, symbolized in the United Nations, in the buildings in Brasilia, and for me perhaps most of all in the 1964 New York World's Fair, was a dream that never came to fruition. It began unraveling in 1963 with the murder of President Kennedy, who seemed perfectly cast to lead us into a refreshing era of high modernity. His successor, by contrast, was a Texas hick and old-time Depression pol who seemed to have fallen right off the tailgate of the Joads' truck. What followed was the patent failure of the expensive Great Society, the incomprehensible Vietnam War, hippies, the counterculture, and economic collapse, all of which forestalled the high-modernist scheme.

Still, in spite of all of this, something about modernism and high modernism beckons to me, especially in poetry. I have a love for the short, lucid poem exhibiting a startling geometric regularity on the page—as obdurate and lasting an object as a cube of concrete. In this way, high modernism was to my mind securely linked to the classical, which exalted what was universal to all of humanity—proportion, reason, justice, and above all, a yearning for the true. As Thoreau noted:

> I know of no studies so composing as those of the classical scholar. When we have sat down to them [the classics], life seems as still and serene as if it were very far off, and I believe it is not habitually seen from any common platform so truly and unexaggerated as in the light of literature. In serene hours we contemplate the tour of the Greek and Latin authors with more pleasure than the traveler does the fairest scenery of Greece or Italy. Where shall we find a more refined society? That highway down from Homer and Hesiod to Horace and Juvenal is more attractive than the Appian. Reading the classics, or conversing with those old Greeks and Latins in their surviving works, is like walking amid the stars and constellations, a high and by-way serene to travel. Indeed, the true scholar will be not a little of an astronomer in his habits. Distracting cares will not be allowed to obstruct the field of his vision, for the higher regions of literature, like astronomy, are above storm and darkness.

Because it tends toward what is universal in both content and form, classical literature has the air of eternity about it. In spite of its antiquity, it seems timeless, unlike for instance, the Bible, which strikes us as anchored in time. As Thoreau himself remarked about Anacreon, "There is something strangely modern about him," which might be said about much of the best classical literature.

The laudable goal of high modernism was to create a new classicism for the twentieth century and beyond. It seems to have achieved it but did so by forsaking something of the human warmth that pervades much classical literature, art, and architecture. To be sure, high modernism allows one to walk amid the stars and constellations, but one finds the atmosphere a bit too cold and airless—its very austerity a kind of exaggeration. Karen Downing's work, by contrast, with its subtle emphasis on the personal, seems to overcome this problem. I realized this—viscerally more than intellectually—after seeing her pottery in Philadelphia.

What I Learned and How I Applied It

So I returned home from the City of Brotherly Love with two things that set me on the path to writing the next four self-symphonies—a snippet of a poem and the realization that there were ways of incorporating the universal and the individual, the formal and the emotional, the ideal and the real in single works that could achieve contemporary relevance. But I was not yet quite sure what to do with this information.

For some reason that I still do not understand, when I next looked at the six lines about the dream of unburying the rabbit, they seemed to me analogous to the scherzo section of a typical four-movement symphony. It was a notion that jumped into my head without any real rational thought behind it. The draft poem's subject matter, which was rather morbid, did not lend itself readily to the idea of celebratory dance or even to the more sobering marches that sometimes constitute the third movement of a symphony. In fact, there was no real correlation between the dead rabbit fragment and symphonic movements at all, let alone the lively pieces generally reserved for a third movement. The only possible connection was the regular end rhyme, which imposed the more systematic rhythm associated with scherzo or march tempos. But the notion of these lines as part of a larger whole analogous to a symphony, in spite of its patent ludicrousness, had sprung into my mind as a kind of inspiration, so I did what any good poet would—I went with it. I wrote four more rhyming lines to augment the rabbit/scherzo section and then set it like a morbid little jewel amid three unrhymed movements. In this way, the second self-symphony was born. I have not included it in the current book, though, because it lacks any connection to the work of Johannes Brahms and therefore does not seem part of this set.

It was only in August 2006 that I decided to do an entire series of musically inspired self-symphonies, and it seemed fitting to return to Brahms to do it. One advantage to using Brahms as an inspiration is that he only composed four symphonies—a doable number, especially since I already had one in hand. There was no reason that I could not have used three additional symphonies by three different composers. But I arbitrarily chose a certain degree of uniformity over diversity. Another reason to use the four Brahms symphonies was temporal. Haydn, Mozart, and Beethoven were much more distant from me in time. Brahms's symphonies, though, had appeared from 1878 to 1885, on the cusp of a modernity that I understood. He seemed a transitional figure, embodying the classicism of Mozart and early Beethoven as well as the Romantic feeling of his mentor Schumann and of the late Beethoven. Moreover, he pointed forward to the more avant-garde possibilities of Schoenberg in the twentieth century. Brahms's music also seemed to blend some of the same elements as Karen Downing's ceramics—classical forms, individual expression, a reflection of experience in the world, and a sense of modernity. This last is particularly present for me in the swirling opening of his First Symphony, which seems almost like the build up to a tragic cataclysm of the kind only the twentieth century could bring. Interestingly, too, Brahms only began to write symphonies when he was forty-four, which was my own age when I wrote the first two self-symphonies.

Having decided how to proceed, I wrote the remaining self-symphonies in order, skipping, of course, the Third, which I had already done. I did the First in the living room in the summer of 2006, but after this decided that changes of scenery were needed for the remaining two. I had read in Walter Niemann's critical biography that Brahms had composed his Second Symphony in the summer of 1877 during his stay at Pörtschach, a bathing resort on the Wörther See, the largest lake in Carinthia. Taking this as a cue, I took my portable music player to the Breakwater Beach Club in Long Branch, New Jersey, and listened to Brahms's Second Symphony, taking in the images from a typical summer beach resort as I composed my poem. This was in the summer of 2007. I opted to write the last self-symphony, inspired by Brahms's Fourth, in an urban setting. I accordingly took the North Jersey Coast Line up to New York and then walked down to Greenwich Village from Penn Station to find an appropriate setting. I was on the lookout, once I passed 14th Street, for a bar or restaurant that had good beer but also sidewalk seating so that I could observe the street life of the city while I listened to Brahms and composed the final self-symphony. I had a difficult time finding a suitable place but finally discovered a bar on a side street that, while it had no sidewalk seating, was otherwise open to the street. I took out my portable music player, put on my earphones, got out my pad and pen, and started to write. But two problems suddenly presented themselves. Soon after I began listening to the Fourth Symphony, the bar, which had been quiet to that point, began to blast some Eric Clapton at a deafening volume. I tried the best I could to soldier through, in spite of the difficulty of hearing Brahms, but after a time, my music player malfunctioned, and I gave up the effort. In spite of these troubles, I did find that I had some good writing but concluded nonetheless that to complete my task required a second trip to the city. This time, I got through the whole symphony with no problem. But I now had the equivalent of one and two-thirds self-symphonies. For the fourth self-symphony, then, I violated my initial rule, which was to write through the whole symphony at a single sitting and to stop when the music stopped, using whatever resulted as a first draft. I decided to use all of the material at hand, but instead of shaping the two drafts I had into two separate poems, I synthesized them into a single self-symphony. In this way, the last of the self-symphonies is distinct in the way it was composed. But all of the material in the original synthesized draft was composed as I listened to Brahms's Fourth, so in that regard, I did not violate my original intention.

My hope is that the methodology I used in creating the self-symphonies will lend them something of its novelty and interest, so that they have become something new, something that didn't exist before. I hope, too, that in their own way they have bridged a gap between the universal and the particular. They also, I think, connect to the classical, but in their own way, not through poetic form, but through their more subtle connection to Brahms's own classicism, picking up from his works a different kind of measure altogether, one that is both classical and modern. In some ways, the self-symphonies reflect the same concerns as Karen Downing's ceramics, but with this reversal: In Karen's work, the formal connection to high modernism and to universalism is most immediately apparent, while individual expressiveness and the variations it produces are more subtly revealed. In the self-symphonies, the individualistic—what is located temporally and spatially—is most readily apparent, while the classical, the universal, the formal, and the high-modernistic elements play somewhere just below the surface.

—D.W.
Eatontown, N.J.
May 9, 2014

ABOUT THE AUTHOR

Daniel Weeks has published six collections of poetry—*X Poems* (Blast Press, 1990), *Ancestral Songs* (Libra Publishers, Inc., 1992), *Indignities* (Mellen Poetry Press, 1999), *Small Beer* (Blast Press, 2007), *Characters* (Blast Press, 2008), and *Virginia* (Blast Press, 2009). In 2013, Blast Press published *Les Symbolistes,* a collection of his French translations. Weeks is also the author of *Not for Filthy Lucre's Sake: Richard Saltar and the Antiproprietary Movement in East New Jersey, 1665-1707,* a history of colonial New Jersey politics, which Lehigh University Press published in 2001. He has received four grants from the New Jersey Historical Commission for research on New Jersey colonial history. His poetry has appeared in *The Cimarron Review, Pebble Lake Review, The California Quarterly, Mudfish, Puckerbrush Review, Zone 3, Slant, The Raintown Review, Barbaric Yawp, The Northwest Florida Review, The Roanoke Review, Sulphur River Literary Review, Mobius, NY Arts Weekly,* and many other publications. Two of his poems were also published in *Wild Poets of Ecstasy: An Anthology of Ecstatic Poetry* (Pelican Pond, 2011). His translations of French symbolist poetry have appeared in *Blue Unicorn.*

Weeks earned a Ph.D. in American history from Rutgers University in 2012. He also holds an M.A. in history from Monmouth University (1995) and a B.A. in American history from Washington & Lee University (1980). He is currently an assistant research professor at the Thomas A. Edison Papers, Rutgers University, and resides in Eatontown, N.J.

Some of Mr. Weeks' books can be purchased from his Amazon author page at:
http://amazon.com/author/danielweeks

ABOUT THE PUBLISHER

BLAST

Meet Me in Botswana: What is BLAST PRESS?

*A speech for national poetry month
about BLAST PRESS by Gregg Glory*

Ab li dolen in l'air [look up: beauty falls from the air]
"A book should be a ball of light in your hands."
~~ Ezra Pound

    As we all know, April is "International Guitar
Month." But my heart twangs for poetry, and I was invited
here to tell you a little bit about a tiny poetry publishing
company called BLAST PRESS.

Let's start with what BLAST PRESS is not. BLAST PRESS is not a community. It is not a community-building venture. It is not by, about, or for "the people." Unlike the pretentious anthologies that weigh down university shelves and slander the individual by gluing him into some historian's scripted story, BLAST PRESS is not a collection of individual voices expressing the vibrancy, meaning, and tradition of the creative community—nor of any community. In this respect, BLAST PRESS, as its critics have bitterly asserted, is nothing at all.

BLAST PRESS has published over 100 chapbooks and softbacks by some thirty authors over the past quarter century. Each author's work stands singularly alone and apart. BLAST PRESS does not take part in the mish-mosh of the magazine market, where a hundred tentative voices are corralled by brute binding into an ersatz herd. We go alone, each of us, to where the crocs swim alertly in the bulrushes and the nights are long. Meet me in Botswana, if you will meet with me at all.

What is a chapbook? A chapbook is a saddle-stapled booklet of plain paper stock folded in half with a sheet of colored card stock for a cover. In the first decade, booklets would be stapled together by hand, each staple closed with a bloody fingertip to save the two-cent per staple cost. All small publishers are unified in this regard: we are exceedingly cheap.

In the next few minutes, for a brief moment, we will hear the voices of some poets that have been published by BLAST PRESS. Their words have been put into chapbooks with a BLAST PRESS logo on the back, and my current address somewhere inside the front flap. Words torn from the air and swatted into print. That is all. But, that is everything.

BLAST PRESS catalog available at:
amazon.com/author/gregglory
and gregglory.com

www.ingramcontent.com/pod-product-compliance
Lightning Source LLC
Chambersburg PA
CBHW081631040426

42449CB00014B/3266